THE OFFICIAL
RANGERS FOOTBALL CLUB
ANNUAL 2019

Written by Paul Kiddie
Designed by Mathew Whittles

A Grange Publication

© 2018. Published by Grange Communications Ltd., Edinburgh, under licence from Rangers Football Club. Printed in the EU.

Photographs © PA Images

ISBN 978-1-912595-17-4

CONTENTS

5

WELCOME

TO THE OFFICIAL RANGERS ANNUAL 2019

It was a tremendous honour to be appointed as the club's manager and I'm thoroughly enjoying being part of the Rangers family.

My team and I are committed to bringing the good times back to Ibrox and giving you, our magnificent supporters, plenty to cheer about. That is the least you deserve and we will work tirelessly to achieve that aim.

Growing up as a kid, I lived and breathed football and enjoyed reading all about my favourite players, whether that be at club level or on the international stage.

We all know the players from watching them on the television or being in the stands for games. But every fan wants to learn something a bit more about the players and the club which mean so much to them.

That's why the Official Rangers Annual 2019 is an important part of any football supporters' collection over the season – and I'm sure you're going to enjoy this year's publication.

Once again it is packed with stories, photographs and interviews with Rangers stars from the past and the present, including some very well-known names such as Mark Hateley and Barry Ferguson.

We all know what a big part they played in the success of the club down the years and I'm sure you'll enjoy reading about their time at Ibrox.

There is a section on first-team player profiles and a chat with my assistant Gary McAllister, someone who I know very well and I was delighted when he agreed to join me here. Throw in some fun puzzles and quizzes to get your mind thinking and I'm sure you won't be able to put the annual down!

Thanks again for your support and I look forward to seeing you at a game very soon.

Steven Gerrard

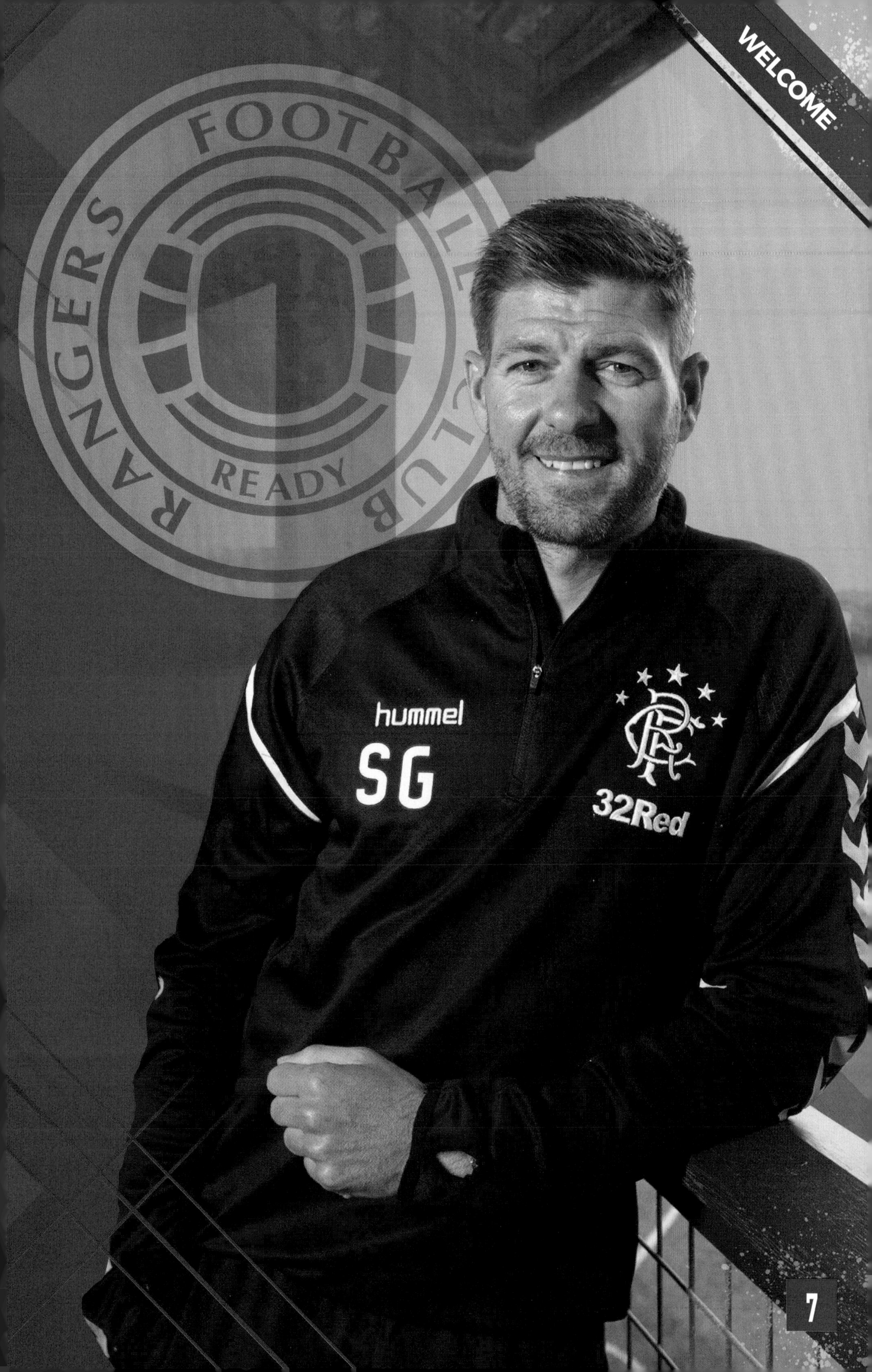
RANGERS FOOTBALL CLUB
READY
hummel
SG
32Red

PLAYER PROFILES

GOALKEEPERS

WES FODERINGHAM

The consistency between the posts shown by the Englishman was a highlight of last season. Time and again the keeper provided a formidable last line of defence for the Light Blues. He started his career at Fulham before signing his first professional contract with Crystal Palace in August 2010. He was loaned out to a number of clubs to gain experience before moving to Swindon where he spent four years. Rangers tempted him north of the Border in 2015.

ALLAN McGREGOR

The Scotland international returned to the club for a second spell in the summer, penning a two-year contract to become Steven Gerrard's second signing. The goalkeeper began his career at Ibrox and had loan spells with St Johnstone and Dunfermline Athletic before pinning down a regular first-team place. In his first spell with Rangers he won 11 major trophies, including three league Championships. He left in 2012 after more than ten years at the club to join Besiktas, from where he moved to Hull City 12 months later. He was named Hull's Player of the Season last term but turned down a contract extension to return to Govan.

DEFENDERS

CONNOR GOLDSON

The central defender penned a four-year contract with the club after leaving Brighton in the summer. Although under contract with the Seagulls until 2020, the boyhood Liverpool fan jumped at the chance to pursue his career under the guidance of Steven Gerrard. Goldson moved to Brighton from Shrewsbury Town in 2015.

DEFENDERS (continued)

JAMES TAVERNIER

The right-back's value to the team was underlined when Steven Gerrard made him captain for the start of the 2018/19 season, the defender having impressed the manager since taking charge in the summer. ▶ The defender lead by example in his boss' first game in charge when he scored in the 2-0 win over Shkupi in the first leg of the Europa League first qualifying round – his first match as skipper. ▶ Tavernier joined the Ibrox side in July 2015 and made an instant impression with a goal on his debut against Hibernian in a Challenge Cup just five days later. ▶ Tavernier won the John Greig Achievement Award at the Player of the Year Ceremony.

BORNA BARIŠIĆ

The full-back was playing for Osijek against Rangers in a Europa League qualifying match when he impressed Steven Gerrard to the extent that the manager brought him to Ibrox on a four year contract just weeks later. ▶ The Croatian international is a class act and was included in the initial 32-man pool for the World Cup in Russia, having already been capped three times for his country.

JON FLANAGAN

The ex-Liverpool defender signed a two year deal in the summer to link up again with former Anfield teammate Steven Gerrard. The full-back made one appearance for Liverpool last season before joining Bolton Wanderers on loan in the English Championship. ▶ Flanagan has represented England on one occasion, when he came off the bench to replace Alex Oxlade-Chamberlain midway through the second half of a 2-2 draw against Ecuador in a 2014 friendly.

NIKOLA KATIĆ

The young Croatian has committed his future to Rangers until 2022 after signing a four-year contract upon leaving Slaven Belupo in his homeland. ▶ The highly rated 6ft 4in centre half was capped for the first time by his country against Mexico in a friendly in May 2017. ▶ He is the fourth Croatian to play for Rangers, following in the footsteps of Dado Pršo, Nikica Jelavić and Niko Kranjčar.

DEFENDERS (continued)

ROSS McCRORIE

The Scotland youth international is another youngster for whom the club has high hopes after he was promoted to the First Team from the Youth Academy. He earned rave reviews for his performance against Aberdeen at the end of the last campaign, his headed equaliser earning the Light Blues a valuable point.

LEE WALLACE

The club's decision to sign the defender from Heart of Midlothian in 2011 for £1.5 million proved a good move, with the left-back quickly cementing a place in the team. He managed his first Old Firm goal with a fabulous finish in Rangers' 3-2 victory over Celtic in March 2012. A Scotland international with plenty of experience, he made his first full international appearance against Japan in October 2009, having previously represented his country at Under-19, Under-20 and Under-21 levels.

JOE WORRALL

An England Under-21 defender, he was brought to the club from Nottingham Forest on a season-long loan. He has played over 50 games for the English Championship side but Steven Gerrard made his move after the stopper failed to feature in any of Forest's games this season. Joe will be hoping his switch to Glasgow will keep him in the picture for more international recognition.

MIDFIELDERS

LASSANA COULIBALY

A Mali international, the midfielder was signed on a season-long loan in the summer from French top flight side Angers. He joined Angers in 2015 from French rivals Bastia and made 48 appearances for the club.

MIDFIELDERS (continued)

SCOTT ARFIELD

Steven Gerrard made the Canadian international his first signing when he brought the striker to Ibrox on a four-year contract. ▶ Born in West Lothian, he began his career with Falkirk before earning a move to Huddersfield Town, following this move with a transfer to Burnley. ▶ The midfielder spent five years with the Lancashire outfit before joining Rangers when his contract at Turf Moor expired. ▶ He represented Scotland at under-19, under-21 and B level but pledged his international allegiance to Canada - his dad was born in Toronto – and won his first cap against Mexico in 2016.

GRAHAM DORRANS

Signing for Rangers in 2017 was a dream come true for the boyhood Gers fan, the midfielder arriving from Norwich on a three-year contract in 2017. ▶ After a good start to the season, injury blighted his season last term, ankle surgery in December ruling him out of action for three months. ▶ A full Scotland international, he also played at the 2006 UEFA Under-19 Championships, where he scored in the 2-1 final defeat to Spain, before going on to represent his nation the following summer at the Under-20 World Cup.

OVIE EJARIA

Manager Steven Gerrard returned to his former club to bring the midfielder to Ibrox on a season-long loan. A versatile player, he can also be deployed as a forward. ▶ A Liverpool player since 2014, Ejaria was on loan at Sunderland last season, where he made 11 appearances. ▶ Currently on a long-term contract at Anfield, he was a member of the England squad that won the Under-20 World Cup in South Korea in 2017.

ANDY HALLIDAY

A boyhood Rangers supporter, he started his senior career with Livingston after being a member of the Rangers Academy until he was 15 years old. ▶ He was delighted to make a return to Govan when Rangers signed him from Bradford City in July 2015. ▶ Last season saw him return early from a loan move to Gabala in Azerbaijan and he's focused on making the most of a second opportunity.

MIDFIELDERS (continued)

RYAN JACK

The former Aberdeen captain moved to Ibrox on a free transfer following the end of his contract at Pittodrie, signing a three-year deal with Rangers. Injury curtailed his involvement, with knee surgery ruling him out of the latter half of the campaign. Jack has had an excellent start to the new season under Steven Gerrard, which he'll hope to build on through 2018/19.

JORDAN ROSSITER

The England youth international had been courted by a number of top clubs while with Liverpool before electing to join the Gers on a four-year deal in 2016. Following a return from injury, Rossiter scored his first Rangers goal in the final game of last season against Hibs. The Scouser will be keen to impress his new boss and former Anfield teammate Steven Gerrard this season.

EROS GREZDA

Having signed the Albanian winger on a four-year contract, Steven Gerrard is expecting the former Osijek wide man to provide a real cutting edge to the Light Blues' attack. Grezda did not feature in Osijek's recent Europa League qualifying matches against the Ibrox outfit because of injury but the manager is confident that signing No. 14 will prove a real fans' favourite during his time with the club.

FORWARDS

ALFREDO MORELOS

The striker created a little bit of Rangers history when he became the first Colombian to sign for the Light Blues in 2017. His form last season in front of goal earned him 18 goals and a finish as the club's joint top scorer. He also earned a nomination for PFA Scotland's Young Player of the Year. In March 2018 he signed a new contract which saw him commit his future to Ibrox until 2021.

FORWARDS (continued)

DANIEL CANDEIAS

Normally deployed as a winger, he showed his versatility when new boss Steven Gerrard played him in a central midfield role early in the season. His tireless work ethic and ability to deliver dangerous crosses were big hits with supporters last season and the former Benefica man was delighted to sign a new two-and-a-half-year contract in March 2018, after winning Player of the Year last season.

RYAN KENT

A graduate of the Liverpool Academy, the winger joined Rangers on a season-long loan from Anfield in July. He signed a long-term contract under Jürgen Klopp in 2017, having made his competitive debut in the FA Cup against Exeter City in 2015. He has had loan spells at Freiburg in Germany as well as with Coventry City, Barnsley and Bristol City. The youngster has also been capped at both Under-18 and Under-20 levels for England.

GLENN MIDDLETON

The Scotland youth international joined from Norwich on a two-and-a-half-year deal early in 2018. Regarded as one of the country's brightest young talents, the winger made his first-team debut when he came off the bench in the 2-0 Europa League first qualifying round, first-leg win over Shkupi at Ibrox, Steven Gerrard's first match in charge.

JAMIE MURPHY

The winger initially joined Rangers on loan from Brighton last January and scored five goals in 19 appearances. He made the move permanent in the summer when he signed a three-year deal. He spent six years at Motherwell before joining Sheffield United in January 2013. He joined Brighton in the summer of 2015 and helped the team compete in the Premier League last year, after they won promotion the season before.

SADIQ UMAR

The Nigerian striker was another player brought to the club by Steven Gerrard on a loan deal. After joining Roma in 2015, he was loaned out to Bologna and Torino and also enjoyed another loan spell with Dutch aces NAC Breda last season. He has scored six goals for his parent club and was in the Nigeria squad that won Bronze at the 2016 Olympic Games in Rio.

FORWARDS (continued)

SERGE ATAKAYI

Born in the DR Congo, the forward joined Rangers from FF Jaro in his adopted homeland of Finland ahead of the 2016/2017 season after a trial with Leicester City.   He signed a three-year contract at the time and has since agreed an extension which will keep him at the club until the summer of 2020.   He became the youngest goalscorer in the history of the Finnish top flight when he scored at the age of 16 years and 107 days.

KYLE LAFFERTY

Kyle Lafferty said he felt like he had come back 'home' after signing for the club for a second time in August.   The striker left Ibrox in 2012 having won three league titles, two Scottish League Cups and a Scottish Cup in his first four-year spell in Govan.   The Northern Ireland international front man signed a two-year deal after leaving Hearts and made his second debut for the Light Blues when he came off the bench in the first leg of the Europa League play-off against FC Ufa at Ibrox.

PLAYERS ON LOAN

ZAK RUDDEN

A regular scorer for the Rangers Academy last season, it didn't take the young striker long to make an impression on new boss Steven Gerrard and his backroom team.   The teenager is unlikely to forget his first pre-season with the club, with the manager having taken him to the club's training camp in the south of Spain.

EDUARDO HERRERA

The Mexico international signed a three-year deal in the summer of 2017, the striker joining from Pumas, and he is currently on loan with Santos Laguna.   He scored twice in 24 games for Rangers, with his last appearance coming off the bench in the Scottish Cup win over Ayr United in February 2018.   Herrera was capped for the first time by Mexico in March 2015 and scored his first international goal in a friendly against Paraguay.

JAK ALNWICK

The former England Under-18 international penned a three-and-a-half year contract in January 2017 after arriving from Port Vale.   He had to wait patiently for his chance and, although he has made only a handful of appearances since arriving at Ibrox, he has proved a capable understudy whenever opportunities have come his way.

PLAYERS ON LOAN (continued)

CARLOS PEÑA (ON LOAN)

The Mexican signed a three-year deal in the summer of 2017 but struggled to make an impression with the First Team. He decided to try his luck away from Ibrox and is currently on loan with Mexican side Necaxa.

LEE HODSON (ON LOAN)

The Northern Ireland international agreed a three-year deal after returning from his country's European Championship campaign in France in 2016. The former MK Dons defender featured five times last season for the First Team.

JAMIE BARJONAS (ON LOAN)

A product of the Rangers Academy, which he joined when still at primary school, Jamie has progressed well through the various age groups. He made his top-team debut in May 2017 when he came off the bench against Partick Thistle at Firhill. The midfielder was delighted to sign a new two-year deal at the end of 2017.

GREG DOCHERTY (ON LOAN)

The former Hamilton midfielder put pen to paper on a four-and-a-half-year contract in January 2018 and produced some encouraging performances early in his Ibrox career. He is currently on loan with Shrewsbury Town.

JOE DODOO (ON LOAN)

The attacker arrived from English Premier League champions Leicester City on a four-year deal in the summer of 2016. Eligible to play for both Ghana and England, Dodoo has represented the Three Lions at youth level previously and is currently on loan at Blackpool.

RYAN HARDIE (ON LOAN)

The 21-year-old benefited from a number of loan moves as he built up his competitive edge and his displays while away from Ibrox, and was rewarded with a new contract keeping him at the club until the summer of 2019. The front man made his professional debut for Rangers in the 2014/15 League Cup when he came off the bench against Falkirk in a 3-1 victory. He marked his first start for Rangers in the best possible fashion, netting twice at Dumbarton in April 2015. The boyhood Rangers fan has represented Scotland at various age levels.

PLAYERS
WORDSEARCH

M	W	C	B	V	B	G	Z	N
O	Q	O	D	R	H	I	T	R
O	S	T	O	G	Z	E	R	E
R	W	U	U	D	T	R	E	P
E	R	O	R	N	S	G	B	O
N	G	H	O	O	Z	P	L	O
T	V	V	J	T	M	F	A	C
M	O	P	A	R	L	A	N	E
N	O	S	R	E	D	N	E	H

Can you find the ten Rangers stars in the grid?

Words can go horizontally, vertically and diagonally
in all eight directions. **Answers on page 61.**

- ☐ Albertz
- ☐ Amoruso
- ☐ Cooper
- ☐ Gough
- ☐ Greig
- ☐ Henderson
- ☐ Moore
- ☐ Novo
- ☐ Parlane
- ☐ Woods

SPOT THE BALL

Can you spot which is the real football in the pictures below?
Answers on page 61.

17

G-FORCE
HITS IBROX

FAN-TASTIC
Thousands of supporters descended on Ibrox to see Steven Gerrard unveiled as the new manager.

LEADER OF THE PACK
The new gaffer brings a vast amount of experience to the dressing-room.

CONTRACT THRILLER

The Rangers board pulled off a major coup when they brought Steven Gerrard to Ibrox as manager.

BIG NEWS

The appointment of Steven Gerrard as Rangers boss was a huge talking point.

SMILES BETTER

The new boss is looking forward to transforming Rangers' fortunes on the park.

LEGEND
LEADS FROM THE FRONT

While the word legend is often thrown around with little justification, there is no doubt that it applies to Steven Gerrard, who accepted the challenge of his first managerial role when he took the reins at Ibrox.

Throughout an illustrious playing career with Liverpool and England, he proved to be an inspirational figure, a leader of men.

A player admired by both teammates and opponents, few will ever match the legacy he carved out at Anfield during a glittering 17-year career.

The only player in Reds history to feature in the club's All-Time Top Five for both appearances and goals, the talismanic midfielder racked up 710 games, scoring 186 goals – uniquely finding the target in the finals of the Champions League, UEFA Cup, FA Cup and League Cup.

His roll of honour at club level speaks for itself: two FA Cups, three League Cups, one Champions League, one UEFA Cup, one UEFA Super Cup and one Community Shield.

Now focused on bringing success back to Rangers, the footballing idol can call on a rich mixture of experience from a number of the managers he played under, as Gerrard explained:

"Rafa Benítez was a fine tactical coach, of course you take a lot from him," he said.

"Then there was Capello at England and Brendan Rodgers in terms of dominating the ball - so I'm blessed in terms of the experience and knowledge I've gained working with those people.

"But the key thing for me is doing it my way and trying to add all the good bits from all those managers to what I've already got.

"I liked one-on-one talks with managers away from the training ground, where I had footage and analysis where I had footage and analysis I could go through for my own game.

"I think it is key for players to see what they do on a football pitch. I think we're in a culture where a lot of coaches use Premier League players and world-class players to show the kids different ideas – which is good, which is fine – but I also think it's important to show them what they do themselves.

"Every player is different, I think there is a risk that players try to emulate and copy a certain player. I think they have to be the player that they are, and learn from the mistakes they're making in a game in order to improve."

On the international stage, Gerrard is the third Most Capped Player for England behind Peter Shilton (125) and David Beckham (115).

He scored 21 goals in his 114 appearances after making his debut in 2000 in a 2-0 win over Ukraine at Wembley and featured in six major tournaments, three of them as skipper.

In all, Gerrard played 12 World Cup Final matches, scoring three goals. His total of 38 matches as skipper has him ranked fifth in the All-Time list behind Bobby Moore, Billy Wright, Bryan Robson and David Beckham.

INTERNATIONAL STATS

Caps: 114

Debut: 31st May 2000 v Ukraine in Wembley friendly (age 20)

Goals: 21

First Goal: 1st September 2001 v Germany in World Cup Qualifier, Munich

Captaincies: 38

Tournaments: Euro 2000, Euro 2004, World Cup 2006, World Cup 2010, Euro 2012 and World Cup 2014

Last Match: 24th June 2014 v Costa Rica in World Cup Finals in Belo Horizonte

GARY McALLISTER

Mac delighted to finally be at Ibrox

Assistant Manager Gary McAllister is loving life as a Light Blue after finally making it to Ibrox.

The former Scotland star had no hesitation in accepting the invitation from Steven Gerrard to join his backroom team in the summer.

But had Lady Luck dealt him a different deck of cards during his playing career, the ex-Liverpool star could well have been directing affairs from the middle of the park years ago.

He said: "There were a few occasions, way back when I started as a boy at Motherwell. Jock Wallace was there and then when he went back to Rangers, I think there was interest in taking me.

" I think to be a player at the highest level everything you do is in and around discipline and that willingness to work hard."

"Then there was a period when I was captain of Leeds United and Scotland, when I think Walter Smith might have been interested.

"I have never actually pinned him down to ask him but there was interest, it was nearly close a couple of times.

"When you get to where I am in life I thought maybe coming here had gone but it is strange how it works."

While delighted to be back at the sharp end, the former Scotland star admitted it took something special to lure him into such a high-profile position.

And after being asked the question, he didn't want to reject the approach only to regret the decision.

"The lure of the club, the profile of the club, means it is one of the few jobs in all honesty that I would have come back into," he said.

"The thing with this job offer was getting another ten years down the line and saying: 'why didn't I take that opportunity at Rangers?'

" The lure of the club, the profile of the club, means it is one of the few jobs in all honesty that I would have come back into."

"I am really enthusiastic about it, it has been really refreshing coming back into the frontline of football again.

"My experience of playing at clubs like this is when you have got everyone together: the fan base, the owners, the coaches and the team, when it gathers momentum anything can happen.

"These clubs can become a juggernaut."

Ironically, it was some words of initial advice from Gary that helped convince Steven that the job of manager was one he couldn't turn down.

The former England international had called his friend to get his thoughts on the job offer and Gary said: "He started off by asking me what I thought of Rangers as a club and in my view Rangers are one of the big, iconic clubs of this country.

"From that point of view it is not dissimilar from Liverpool, which is where he has played most of his life. I was very encouraging for him to take on this challenge.

"I think he had sorted his staff and maybe this opportunity of being his assistant might not have been there and then he was asked who it would be that you might want to bring in to strengthen your ultimate team and he came up with my name.

"When that was the case, first and foremost I was honoured that he asked me but it is about embracing the challenge of this club, coming along here to make a difference.

"I am that go-between the players and the manager, and what Steven wants me to do, it sits really well with me.

"I think discipline is something you expect. I shouldn't need to take on any role like that. Being disciplined shouldn't be a surprise in modern day football.

"I think to be a player at the highest level everything you do is in and around discipline and that willingness to work hard."

He added: "I think if you are looking at me I certainly have more experience; I am fortunate that I have good experience.

"I suppose the facts are that I am more of an old player that players can lean on; I think that is where I see my role. A player who has played a lot of games and played at a lot of different types of club and I have represented my country.

"You have Steven who has jumped straight into the coaching side of things, immediately he has taken the pathway of working with younger players."

Gary forms part of a management team that includes Michael Beale, Tom Culshaw, Jordan Milsom and Colin Stewart.

"Mick Beale is somebody that I have known over the years working at Liverpool, he is a fantastic, very modern coach and he is right at the cutting edge of modern day coaching," he said.

"Tommy (Culshaw) is another guy I have known for years, as is Jordan (Milsom) on the sports science side of things. These guys are not foreign to me, they are very much guys that I know and I know their capabilities."

NO PAIN NO GAIN
PRE-SEASON

For his first pre-season as manager, it was destination Spain for Steven Gerrard.

The boss took his players to the Costa del Sol to run the rule over the squad under the hot Mediterranean sunshine.

Based in Malaga, this was no holiday for the Light Blues, with the gaffer, his assistant Gary McAllister and the rest of his backroom team putting the squad through a punishing series of training sessions.

It was the usual mix of runs, shuttles, circuits and ball work which players generally regard as a necessary evil ahead of the serious competitive action.

Friday, July 6th

Rangers 6-0 Bury

Goals: Murphy, Katic, Arfield (2), Morelos, Rudden

Steven Gerrard enjoyed the best possible start to his reign as Rangers manager with his new-look squad confidently beating English League Two side Bury.

An incredible crowd of 41,015 descended on Ibrox to take in the friendly and were rewarded for their loyalty with the Light Blues in fine form on a glorious night in Govan.

Goals from the impressive Jamie Murphy and debutants Nikola Katic and Scott Arfield put the home side 3-0 up at the break and their dominance continued in the second period with Arfield, Alfredo Morelos and young striker Zak Rudden adding to the scoreline.

RANGERS: McGregor (McCrorie 79), Tavernier (Hodson 72), Goldson (Bradley 79), Katic (Wilson 69), Flanagan (John 45), McCrorie (Jack 62), Windass (Atakayi 72), Candeias (Halliday 62), Arfield (Docherty 69), Murphy (Middleton 62), Morelos (Rudden 72)

Sunday, July 29th

Rangers 3-0 Wigan

Goals: Morelos, Katic, Bruce (og)

Wigan Athletic from the English Championship were swept aside by a much-changed but rampant Rangers side in the Light Blues' final pre-season friendly.

Goals from Alfredo Morelos, Nikola Katic and an Alex Bruce own-goal secured a highly impressive win for Steven Gerrard's side.

The match gave supporters another chance to see their favourites in action and the result kept the momentum going ahead of the first competitive action of the season.

RANGERS: Alnwick (Foderingham, 45) Tavernier (Hodson, 64), Bradley (Katic, 45), Goldson (Coulibaly, 72), Halliday (Murphy, 64), McCrorie, Docherty (Kent, 72), Ejaria (Arfield, 64), Candeias (Kelly 80), Middleton, Morelos (Sadiq, 55).

25

SCOTT'S PERFECT MATCH

Move to Ibrox was just what Arfield needed

When a footballer signs for a club the size of Rangers, there is a unique pressure on that player to perform.

When you are new manager Steven Gerrard's first signing, then it's fair to say that pressure rises a notch or two in tandem with supporters' expectations.

Such a scenario, however, did not faze Scott Arfield, the midfielder relishing the challenge the move to Ibrox represented with his contract at Burnley expiring.

The former Falkirk star didn't have to think about things for too long once he knew the Kop legend was keen to have him on board as part of his exciting rebuilding project at Ibrox.

"If you can't handle the expectation and you don't want to take responsibility then you shouldn't walk through the front door," said Scott, who signed a four-year contract with the Light Blues.

"I'm at a time in my life where I can take that.

"To come to a club this size is perfect for me at this time in my career.

"Loads of people down in England don't realise how big football is up here, but I feel quite secure in my thinking that I know how life is probably going to change.

> ❝ I was lucky enough to play against Steven when I was at Burnley and he was just finishing off at Liverpool."

"It was quite an easy decision, and also an easy decision for me and my family to come back up the road.

"I know Graham Dorrans and Jamie Murphy and spoke to them on a number of occasions. They only said good things.

"I spoke to players who have been at Rangers and Celtic about the off-the-field things your family needs to go through and the pressures of off-the-field living.

"It is something that I have never really had to deal with. I've been in villages and towns and it's not been a problem.

"I obviously know that side of it is going to be under more scrutiny, so I had to make sure I knew how to deal with it. It's not just me signing for Glasgow Rangers. It's everyone associated with me. They know I love them and they love me, so everyone has to be on the same page to make it successful on the pitch."

Gerrard has been the perfect role model for thousands of footballers the length and breadth of the country and Scott is no different.

"When you have a name like that, and also his No. 2 Gary McAllister, it was quite an easy decision," he said.

"I was lucky enough to play against Steven when I was at Burnley and he was just finishing off at Liverpool.

"He's been every midfielder's inspiration I think and he was certainly mine. I'm incredibly lucky that in the next four years I'm going to work with him every day."

After leaving Falkirk in 2010, Arfield joined Huddersfield Town and then Burnley three years later, working his way through the leagues to eventually become a Premier League star.

Scott, capped a dozen times for Canada, feels he has learned so much from every level he has played at.

"Even when I went down to England to League One," he said, "it was a completely different environment to what I was used to when I left Falkirk.

"It's easy to go in the Premier League and you can play so many years and drop down, but I did it in reverse going from League One up.

"It helped so much staying in a different place away from family, and I think the experiences of playing against those top players at Premier League level can only help."

GUESS WHO?

Can you guess who the players are in the portraits below?

Answer on page 61.

JAMES
TAVERNIER

29

MARK OF A LEGEND

Ibrox stay was career highlight for Hateley

Rangers legend Mark Hateley made a lifetime of memories during his playing career at Ibrox – after taking just minutes to decide to join the Glasgow giants.

The striker was struggling through injury at Monaco and hadn't kicked a ball in earnest for two years when Graeme Souness made contact, offering him the chance to kick-start his career with the Light Blues.

It was the summer of 1990 and the then-Rangers manager was staying in Monaco while watching matches at the World Cup in nearby Italy.

Hateley still had three years to run of his contract with Monaco but with his manager Arsène Wenger happy to give his front man the chance to move, things happened very quickly.

> **A deal was literally done with Graeme in ten minutes and the rest is history as they say."**

"I was coming out the back end of a two year injury period at Monaco, when I hadn't played any football and had gone through various operations," said the ex-England international.

"I was focusing on getting myself fit and ready for the 1990 season.

"Graeme and his chairman were staying in Monaco for Italia '90 and that's how it all started. He called me, we had a meeting and they explained where they wanted to take the club. Although, I still had three years to go on my contract with Monaco, I spoke to Arsène Wenger and he was fine about it.

"He said whatever decision I made, he knew I would get back playing how I used to. He did say he thought a change of environment might be good for me, though.

Hateley never looked back after switching to Scotland, his goals and playing style making him a firm favourite with the Rangers fans, none more so than when he hit a double at Ibrox to ensure his team pipped Aberdeen to the title on the last day of the season in 1991, their third of nine-in-a-row.

He said: "That 1990 season was the beginning of a great period in my footballing career and probably one of the happiest times of my playing career.

"I was more or less injury-free and, as Wenger said, a change did bring a change of fortunes.

"The first season was a hard one after a two year lay-off and it took me longer to get back into the swing of things than I thought. The final game of the season against Aberdeen was when it all came together for me with the two goals. After that it was plain sailing and I couldn't wait to get back after the summer and start the new season."

The man who scored over 100 goals for Rangers and won the league every season he pulled on the jersey added: "It was a fantastic experience for me, great to be playing with Alistair and great to be in a team that was absolutely crammed full of world class players, in my eyes anyway.

"It was the right time and the right move for me. I didn't play that much international football but I wasn't bothered about that.

> ❝ What I was bothered about was winning stuff, playing well, scoring goals and creating goals, which we did in sack loads! We went from one success to another, doubles and trebles. It was great."

The ex-England star, who has been a club ambassador for 18 years, enjoyed a brief second stint with the club, famously joining them in 1997 from QPR as nine-in-a-row was achieved, although he managed just four games.

"It took me a nano second to make my mind up to come back. Nine-in-a-row was a happy time indeed!" he said.

He was delighted to see the club lure someone of the calibre of Steven Gerrard to the manager's office and he's confident better times are not far away.

"Rangers is a Scottish institution and has a global capacity to grab fans. We have supporters all over the world and it's as big as it comes," he said.

"We've been to those heights and I'm sure we can get back to those heights again with a little bit of steadiness over the next couple of years with the players of good pedigree that Steven can attract.

"It is a bit like Graeme Souness. He brought the brand, the player, the charisma to Ibrox and it's the same if not more with Steven as he has a bigger profile.

"He's still a young man but has more experience than when 'Souey' came into the club – he hadn't coached and was still playing when he took the job at Ibrox."

RANGERS
CROSSWORD

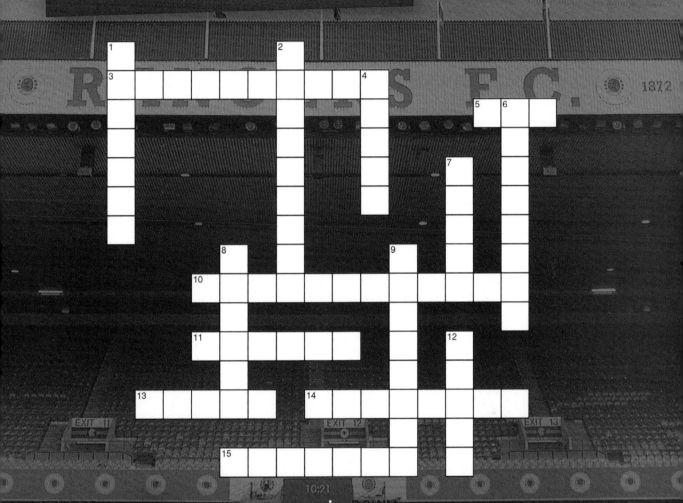

ACROSS

3 Rangers are also known by what name? (5,5)

5 In which month does Steven Gerrard celebrate his birthday? (3)

10 The stand opposite the Ibrox main stand is named after which famous ex-player? (5,7)

11 Former star Jorg Albertz was nicknamed the what? (6)

13 The area of Glasgow where Ibrox is located. (5)

14 Gary McAllister was capped 59 times by which country? (8)

15 In which Merseyside town was the manager born? (7)

DOWN

1 Jak is a star between the posts. (7)

2 Which club did Jason Holt join on loan? (9)

4 First name of Steven Gerrard's first signing. (5)

6 Who provided the opposition for Steven Gerrard's first league game in charge? (8)

7 Can you name Rangers' official club mascot? (5)

8 The Spanish city where Rangers began their pre-season training. (6)

9 Rangers raided which English club to sign Connor Goldson? (8)

12 Rangers defeated Dynamo Moscow to win the European Cup-Winners' Cup in which country? (5)

Answers on page 61.

33

MADE IN ENGLAND

The arrival at Ibrox of former Liverpool and England captain Steven Gerrard sent shock waves through Scottish football. The Kop legend, of course, is not the first high-profile Englishman to walk up the famous marble staircase. Here we take a look at some of the others from south of the Border to become big hits with the supporters.

TERRY BUTCHER

Despite interest from Manchester United and Tottenham Hotspur, Rangers manager Graeme Souness won the race for his signature by forking out a club record fee of £725,000 in 1986.

The English international's arrival from Ipswich Town after the World Cup in Mexico set tongues wagging and sent out a clear message that the Rangers board meant business.

Butcher scored the winning goal against Aberdeen at Pittodrie to clinch the club's first league title in nine years in his first season at the club.

After breaking his leg, he came back into the team to help Rangers win back-to-back League Championships in 1989 and 1990.

He made 176 appearances, scoring 11 goals, before joining Coventry City as player-manager in 1990.

CHRIS WOODS

He was battling it out for the England No. 1 jersey with Peter Shilton when Rangers came calling, the club breaking the British transfer record for a goalkeeper to bring him to Glasgow in the summer of 1986. The club paid £600,000 to secure his services.

Woods was a key member

of the team, playing a vital role in his first full season as the Gers lifted the Premier Division Championship trophy for the first time in nine years.

Woods made a total of 230 appearances for Rangers during his five-year stay, leaving Ibrox in the 1991 close season to join Sheffield Wednesday for £1.2 million.

TREVOR STEVEN

The midfielder had won numerous honours with Everton before he decided to try his luck in Glasgow in 1989 and it's a decision which paid dividends both for him and the club.

The England international enjoyed two spells with the Ibrox club, netting the winner against Dundee United at Tannadice in his first season to capture the Light Blues' second title in succession.

He moved to Olympique Marseille in 1991 for £5.5 million but after one season in France he returned to Rangers in the summer of 1992 and became one of the nine-in-a-row heroes before hanging up his boots in 1997.

MARK WALTERS

With 50 goals in 144 appearances for Rangers, it is easy to see the impact the winger had during his three-and-half-year stay at Ibrox.

He set Scottish football alight after his arrival on Hogmanay 1987, with fans quick to raise a glass to his trickery and ability to turn defences inside out.

His cross for Mark Hateley's famous headed winner at Pittodrie will always be recalled with excitement by supporters.

With three League Championship wins and two League Cups to his credit as a Ger, there is a warm welcome awaiting him any time he comes back to visit.

MARK HATELEY

The powerful attacker was one of the most lethal forwards to pull on the famous Rangers jersey, smashing 115 goals in 222 games for the club after first joining from AS Monaco in 1990.

Hateley was voted Player of the Year, by the Scottish Football Writers Association in the 1993/94 season, becoming the first Englishman to win this prestigious award.

He left Ibrox in 1995 to join QPR and briefly returned to Rangers to help the cause prior to the nine-in-a- row decider at Parkhead.

PAUL GASCOIGNE

Born in Gateshead on May 27 1967, Gascoigne signed for Rangers in July 1995 for £4.3 million and is widely regarded as one of the most talented players to ever grace the Ibrox turf.

By the time he signed on the dotted line in Govan, the midfield genius could already count Newcastle United, Tottenham Hotspur and Lazio among his clubs.

Gazza won 14 of his England caps during his time north of the Border, scoring 39 goals in 103 games for the club.

RAY WILKINS

The £250,000 which Rangers spent on bringing the experienced Wilkins to Ibrox in November 1987 proved money very well spent.

He became a key member of the 'Souness revolution', demonstrating his value with two years of classy consistency.

Capped 84 times for England, he will be fondly remembered for the thunderbolt he scored against Celtic in August 1988 as Rangers romped to a 5-1 triumph.

He won two league titles and a league cup medal in his two-year stay before a return to London for family reasons.

Everyone at the club was stunned to learn of his untimely death in April 2018.

ALL CHANGE
AT TRAINING CENTRE

The winds of change which swept through Ibrox in the summer reached as far as the club's training complex at Auchenhowie, with the facility being renamed the Hummel Training Centre.

The Danish sportswear company is Rangers' new technical kit supplier for the next three seasons and the partnership extended to the naming rights of the 38-acre training centre, which was opened in 2001 at a cost of £14 million.

Allan Vad Nielsen, CEO of Hummel International, said: "We are delighted to be further strengthening our relationship with Rangers Football Club.

"Our decision to take up the naming rights for this great facility was a very easy one; at Hummel we pride ourselves on engaging with players, staff and fans across all levels when working with partner clubs. To add to our brand name to the busy day-to-day hub of this great club ensures we can do just that."

Rangers managing director Stewart Robertson added: "We are committed to working closely with all our partners and sponsors as we enter a new chapter for the club under Steven Gerrard.

"We are looking forward to growing the relationship between our club, our fans and Hummel."

Hummel will produce three bespoke kits each season as well as a range of training wear.

ONES TO WATCH

Throughout the years, Rangers Football Club has been proud to produce some of the country's finest footballers. The conveyor belt of talent shows no signs of stopping and here we focus on another group of up-and-coming youngsters, all on track to make a name for themselves in the game.

Robby McCrorie

The twin brother of fellow Rangers starlet Ross, Robby joined the club in the summer of 2017, after working his way through the Light Blues' youth ranks.

Capped at Under-19 level for Scotland, 6ft 2in keeper Robby is highly-rated and cuts an imposing figure between the sticks.

He performed well while on loan at Berwick Rangers last season and was included in the First Team squad for the pre-season training camp in Spain.

Glenn Middleton

The winger joined Rangers from Norwich City in January 2018 and caught the eye with some impressive displays for the development squad.

Promoted to the First Team squad, Middleton made his competitive debut in the Europa League first qualifying round first-leg tie against Shkupi at Ibrox and coped well with the step up in class to attract lots of praise from onlookers.

He has represented Scotland at a variety of age levels, including the U21s.

Stephen Kelly

Another of the crop of rising stars coming through the Academy, the central midfielder will have benefited enormously from being part of the squad in Spain in the summer.

The teenager came to prominence with his displays for the U20s last term and will be looking to continue that improvement.

He has an eye for goal, is good in possession and has a wide range of passing at his disposal.

Cammy Palmer

The 18 year old is another one of the Academy stars who the club has high hopes for.

Originally from Toronto, the midfielder impressed on a trial while in Glasgow and the club made their move to snap up the promising youngster.

He signed a contract which keeps him at Ibrox until the summer of 2020.

RANGERS
WORDSEARCH

F	F	K	F	Z	D	L	Z	S
O	Y	S	L	A	O	G	E	G
O	D	D	T	R	M	I	X	W
T	A	R	Z	V	H	O	O	F
B	E	A	N	P	R	G	U	F
A	R	R	O	B	S	K	A	S
L	T	R	I	A	C	N	H	X
L	T	E	L	B	S	G	N	Y
W	L	G	Q	G	O	V	A	N

Can you find the ten Rangers words in the grid?

Words can go horizontally, vertically and diagonally in all eight directions.

☐ Famous
☐ Fans
☐ Football
☐ Gerrard
☐ Glasgow
☐ Goals
☐ Govan
☐ Ibrox
☐ Ready
☐ Trophies

Answers on page 61.

ALFREDO
MORELOS

CUP OF CHEER

Trophy joy for young Gers after final flourish

GLASGOW CUP FINAL

Venue: Firhill Stadium
Score: Rangers U17s **3–0** Celtic U17s
Goals: Dickson (2), Kennedy

The 2018 Glasgow Cup was full of cheer for Rangers Under-17s as the Ibrox young guns proved too good for their Celtic rivals.

The youngsters deserved their moment of glory after recording a comfortable 3-0 victory at Firhill against a team which had to play the majority of the game with ten men.

The red card incident happened after just 12 minutes, when Josh McPake was hauled down as he ran in on goal, the decision giving Rangers a vital foothold in the game.

Moments after being handed a numerical advantage, Brian Gilmour's side broke the deadlock from the penalty spot after the referee spotted a handball.

Ciaran Dickson was the player handed the responsibility and he made no mistakes when sending it into the back of the net.

A goal up and a man up, Rangers could sniff the scent of victory and they produced a

RANGERS: Budinauckas, Patterson, Butterworth (O'Connor 84'), Williamson (Yates 84'), Finlayson, McClelland, McPake, Miller, Mebude (Maxwell 70'), Dickson, Kennedy.
Subs not used: Hogarth, Mack, McKinnon, Balde

professional performance to drive home their advantage.

Dickson doubled his side's lead with his second of the game as the half-hour mark approached.

Zac Butterworth's delivery from the left fell at the feet of the young star who showed great footwork to evade his marked player before slamming a shot into the corner of the net.

The Academy aces almost made it three before the break, Dapo Mebude and Kai Kennedy both getting close.

Kennedy didn't have to wait too long to get his name on the scoresheet, however, when he drifted in from the left wing to touch Nathan Patterson's cross beyond the keeper after a superb surging run by the full-back.

The goalscorer then smashed a late chance at keeper Mullen from outside the box and only a great leap from the Celtic man denied the winger, who was superb on the night. Josh McPake followed up that chance when he drilled a strike at Mullen from just a couple of yards out but he hung on to spare further blushes for his side.

The margin of victory could easily have been greater but nonetheless it was an impressive win for the young Gers.

41

Q&A

BARRY FERGUSON

Q MEMORIES OF YOUR DEBUT?

The overriding feeling was just nerves. Rangers had won nine-in-a-row and I made my debut in the last game of that 1996/97 season against Hearts at Tynecastle. Having watched a lot of the players as a supporter and then trained with them, here I was on the same pitch as them and it was a dream come true for me. It was a big thing for my family as well, with my brother Derek also having played for the club he'd supported as a kid.

Q MOST MEMORABLE MATCH PLAYED IN?

There are a number but probably the one which stands out is the Scottish Cup Final in 2002 when we beat Celtic 3-2 at Hampden. Beating your close rivals is always good and

to do it with the last kick of the ball is even sweeter.

Q MOST MEMORABLE MATCH WATCHED?

That would be the time when I was sitting in the stand as a young lad and saw Gazza score a hat-trick to beat Aberdeen 3-0. He was one of my heroes and took that game by the scruff of the neck and scored a wonderful hat-trick.

Q FAVOURITE GOAL?

I have three favourite goals – and it's the three goals I scored against Celtic! To play in one of those games is amazing but to score against your fiercest rivals is something else.

Q TOUGHEST OPPONENT?

That's a difficult one as I came up against a lot of quality players in my time. I would

probably go for Xavi, the former Barcelona and Spain star. Although I was never directly against him on the pitch, he was such a difficult player to read and could disguise a pass brilliantly. He never seemed to lose the ball and had an extraordinary range of passes. I would try to read what he was going to do so he would misplace a pass but it was so difficult. He was so aware of where players were; a wonderful footballer.

Q BEST TEAMMATE?

I would have to say Arthur Numan as he was such a good influence on me as a young boy. I have a lot of friends I still keep in contact with but he was my roommate and was a big help to my development not just as a player but as a person.

Q DRESSING ROOM PRANKSTER?

My vote for dressing-room prankster and all-round pain in the backside goes to Fernando Ricksen. He was always up to something, great fun but a real pain in the butt at the same time.

Q MANAGER MEMORIES?

I was lucky enough to play for some very good managers. I can't single anyone out in front of someone else but the three I learned the most from were Walter Smith, Dick Advocaat and Alex McLeish. I couldn't separate them. There were all good in different ways.

Q FAVOURITE REFEREE?

It would have to be Hugh Dallas. You could give him a bit and he would give you a bit back. It's changed days now in as much as you can't seem to speak to a referee without getting booked. If you gave Hugh a hard time, he gave you a hard time back and that's what I respected about him.

Q EUROPEAN MEMORIES?

Playing in the Champions' League, for me the best

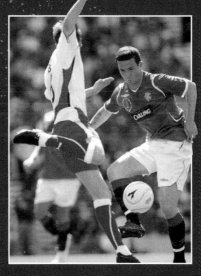

tournament in the world, against some of the top teams' best players and see how I did against them, was a memory in itself. I couldn't highlight one specific memory. People go on about the UEFA Cup run, which was unbelievable at the end of the day, but we didn't win it.

Q ANY SUPERSTITIONS?

I had the same shin guards for nearly 15 years and used to always put my left one on first. I also wore the same pair of boots in every game for three years. I wasn't a big fan of changing boots and kit man Jimmy Bell used to take them to the cobblers to get them put together when required.

Q FAVOURITE FILM?

Scarface

Q FAVOURITE ACTOR?

Al Pacino

Q FAVOURITE ACTRESS?

Sharon Stone

Q FAVOURITE CAR?

A Mini Cooper

Q FAVOURITE PET?

I'm a dog person and although it sounds strange given their difference in size, I'd say a Great Dane or a Pug. I have a Pug at the moment but have also had Great Danes. They are my two favourite breeds.

Q FAVOURITE HOLIDAY?

Beaches don't do it for me. I like nothing better than relaxing by the pool when I'm away on holiday.

Q BEST PIECE OF ADVICE RECEIVED?

My youth coaches John McGregor and John Brown always told me: train the way you want to play. These are simple words but ones which were so important to me throughout my career.

Q WHAT WOULD YOU SAY TO ANY ASPIRING FOOTBALLER?

I would tell them to work their backsides off in training: put everything into training to improve themselves. For me, what you put into training is what you get out of it. I did that from the age of 15 when I went full-time right up to the age of 37.

RANGERS
ROLL OF HONOUR

TITLES

European Cup Winners' Cup
Winners 1972; Runners-up 1961, 1967

UEFA Cup
Runners-up 2008

Scottish League Champions (54)
*1891, 1899, 1900, 1901, 1902, 1911, 1912, 1913,
1918, 1920, 1921, 1923, 1924, 1925, 1927, 1928,
1929, 1930, 1931, 1933, 1934, 1935, 1937, 1939,
1947, 1949, 1950, 1953, 1956, 1957, 1959, 1961,
1963, 1964, 1975, 1976, 1978, 1987, 1989, 1990,
1991, 1992, 1993, 1994, 1995, 1996, 1997, 1999,
2000, 2003, 2005, 2009, 2010, 2011

*In 1891 the Championship was shared
 with Dumbarton

Scottish Cup Winners (33)
1894, 1897, 1898, 1903, 1928, 1930, 1932, 1934,
1935, 1936, 1948, 1949, 1950, 1953, 1960, 1962, 1963,
1964, 1966, 1973, 1976, 1978, 1979, 1981, 1992, 1993,
1996, 1999, 2000, 2002, 2003, 2008, 2009

Scottish League Cup Winners (27)
Season Starting: 1946, 1948, 1960, 1961, 1963,
1964, 1970, 1975, 1977, 1978, 1981, 1983, 1984,
1986, 1987, 1988, 1990, 1992, 1993, 1996, 1998,
2001, 2002, 2004, 2007, 2009, 2010

SPFL Championship Winners (1)
2016

SPFL League One Winners (1)
2014

Scottish Division Three Winners (1)
2013

Scottish Challenge Cup Winners (1)
2016

Scottish League Champions
54 times!

Record Ibrox Attendance
118,730
v Celtic, Division One, January 2nd, 1939

RESULTS

Record Victory
13-0 v Possilpark, Scottish Cup, October 6, 1877;
v Uddingston, Scottish Cup, November 10, 1877
and v Kelvinside, Scottish Cup, September 28, 1889

Most Goals in a Game
14-2 Blairgowrie, Scottish Cup, 1934

Record Defeat
1-7 v Celtic, League Cup Final, October 19, 1957

Record League Victory
10-0 v Hibs, December 24, 1898

Record League Defeat
0-6 v Dumbarton, May 4, 1892

Record Scorer: Ally McCoist
355 goals

PLAYERS

Record Appearances
Dougie Gray, 948, 1925-27

Record League Appearances
Sandy Archibald, 513, 1917-34

Record Scottish Cup Appearances
Alec Smith, 74

Record League Cup Appearances
John Greig, 121

Record European Appearances
Barry Ferguson 82

Record Scorer
Ally McCoist 355 goals, 1983-98

Highest Number of Goals in a Season
Jim Forrest, 57 goals in 1964-65

Highest Number of League Goals in a Season
Sam English, 44 goals in 1931-32

Most League Goals
Ally McCoist, 251

Most Scottish Cup Goals
Jimmy Fleming, 44

Most League Cup Goals
Ally McCoist, 55

Most European Goals
Ally McCoist, 21

Most Capped Player
Ally McCoist [61 caps for Scotland]

Record Transfer Fee Received
£9million received for Alan Hutton

Record Transfer Fee Paid
£12million paid for Tore Andre Flo

Record Victory
13-0

HELP ARFIELD
ESCAPE THE MAZE

Summer signing Scott Arfield was Steven Gerrard's first foray into the transfer market as Rangers manager. Scott was super excited to play his first match at Ibrox for his new club. Can you help him find his way out of the maze to make sure he makes kick-off on time?

KICK OFF!

Answers on page 61.

Ross County 1, Rangers 3
Goals: Morelos (2), Herrera

The month of August kicked off with a great victory away from home and Rangers finished the month off with another fine result on the road, this time in Dingwall.

Alfredo Morelos showed his predatory instincts in front of goal with a first half double to build the foundations for the win.

The home side dragged their way back into things after the break with Thomas Mikkelsen netting and after withstanding plenty of pressure from the Staggies, the visitors made the game safe when Eduardo Herrera grabbed his first goal for the club in the closing minutes.

Scottish Premiership
Motherwell 1, Rangers 2
Goals: Dorrans (2)

Fir Park is never the easiest of venues to get a result so when Rangers opened their league campaign with a victory over the Steelmen in Lanarkshire, the Light Blues' camp could not have been happier.

Graham Dorrans set the ball rolling on his competitive debut when he opened the scoring with just four minutes on the clock.

Although the hosts levelled through Ben Heneghan before the interval, Rangers weren't to be denied and Dorrans slotted home his second of the match from the penalty spot before the hour mark to restore his side's advantage.

It completed a dream debut for the lifelong Gers fan and saw the Rangers squad travel back to Ibrox with a spring in their step.

RANGERS: Foderingham, Tavernier, Cardoso, Alves, Wallace; Candeias, Jack, Dorrans, Kranjcar (Peña 62'), Morelos (Rossiter 78'), Miller (Herrera 60').
Subs not used: Alnwick, Hodson, Wilson, Dálcio.

RANGERS: Foderingham; Hodson (Tavernier 61), Cardoso, Alves, Wallace; Candeias, Jack, Dorrans, Windass; Herrera (Morelos 82), Miller (Wilson 76). Subs not used: Alnwick, Holt, Dálcio, Peña.

Saturday 9th September 2017

Rangers 4, Dundee 1
Goals: Morelos (2), Windass, Peña

Rangers recorded their first home win in the league in some style as they swept aside former star Neil McCann's Dundee side.

Appropriately enough on Armed Forces Day at Ibrox, the hosts put on a display to remember.

Alfredo Morelos grabbed himself another brace, scoring in each half as the Gers produced a performance much appreciated by a packed stadium.

Josh Windass headed home his first goal for the club in the second half and Carlos Peña completed the scoring for Rangers. The visitors netted a consolation effort through Faissal El Bakhtaoui in the closing moments but that failed to take the shine off a polished performance.

RANGERS: Foderingham; Tavernier, Cardoso, Alves, Wallace; Candeias (Nemane, 87), Jack, Dorrans, Kranjcar (Windass, 54); Miller (Peña, 63), Morelos. Subs not used: Alnwick, McCrorie, Herrera, Rossiter.

Friday 29th September 2017

Hamilton Accies 1, Rangers 4
Goals: John (2), Candeias, Dorrans

It was an action packed Friday night as Rangers dished out a heavy defeat, the margin of victory their biggest away win over Accies in more than 50 years.

Things didn't start so well for the visitors, with Hamilton racing into the lead with barely a minute on the clock, Danny Redmond stunning the visitors.

However, within 25 minutes, though, Rangers had taken the lead and it was a special moment for Declan John. The Welshman netted his goal for the club and then levelled proceedings with a superb long-range shot. Moments later, he was celebrating a second goal after evading the home defence. Daniel Candeias scored No. 3 to complete an impressive first-half turnaround.

Despite being a man down after Ryan Jack received a second yellow card in the second half, Rangers stretched their lead from Graham Dorrans' spot-kick after Jason Holt had been fouled in the area.

There was another penalty awarded in the match, this time in favour of the hosts but Wes Foderingham showed his class to keep out Rakish Bingham's effort.

RANGERS: Foderingham; Tavernier, Cardoso, McCrorie, John; Candeias (Dálcio, 90), Jack, Dorrans, Windass; Peña (Holt, 55), Morelos (Herrera, 74).
Subs not used: Alnwick, Hodson, A. Wlson, Nemane.

Friday 13th October 2017

St Johnstone 0, Rangers 3
Goals: Peña (2), Dorrans

Friday night football seemed to be suiting Rangers, with the Light Blues chalking up another impressive result on their travels.

The visitors got their noses in front when Carlos Peña opened the scoring as the half-hour mark approached, the strike Rangers' only effort on target in what was a pretty dull opening 45 minutes.

It was a more lively affair after the break, however. Any hope Saints had of taking something from the game went up the tunnel with skipper Steven Anderson, the captain receiving his second yellow card of the game in the 71st minute.

Seven minutes later, Peña netted his second of the night to make it 2-0 and four minutes from time Graham Dorrans completed the scoring with an accurate low drive into the St Johnstone net.

RANGERS: Foderingham, Tavernier, Cardoso, Alves, John, Dorrans, Holt, Peña (McCrorie 85'), Candeias, Morelos (Herrera 87'), Windass (Nemane 90'). Subs not used: Alnwick, Hodson, Barjonas, Dálcio.

Saturday 28th October 2017

Hearts 1, Rangers 3
Goals: Miller (2), Windass

This was a milestone fixture for the club, with Rangers visiting Murrayfield for the first time to take on Hearts, who had decanted to the home of Scottish Rugby during a major ground upgrade at Tynecastle.

The visitors marked the occasion with an important win to send the 14,000 supporters who had made the journey east back home along the M8 in good spirits.

Things didn't start too well, though, with Kyle Lafferty putting Hearts ahead in the first half. Kenny Miller popped up with an equaliser before the interval and added a second after the break to hand Gers the advantage. Josh Windass completed the scoring to round off a good afternoon's work.

RANGERS: Foderingham, Tavernier, John, Wilson, Jack, Miller (Barjonas, 84), Windass (Hardie, 90), Morelos (Herrera, 87), Candeias, Holt, McCrorie. Subs not used: Kelly, Hodson, Kranjcar, Bates.

Rangers 3, Partick Thistle 0
Goals: McCrorie, Candeias, Windass

The excellent win over Hearts was followed up seven days later with another victory, this time Partick Thistle being put to the sword at Ibrox.

It was a special day for young Ross McCrorie, who put the hosts ahead with his first goal for the club on the half-hour mark, an unstoppable header high into the net.

Two goals either side of the break made the game safe for Rangers. Daniel Candeias popped up in the 39th minute to double the advantage before Josh Windass got his name on the scoresheet once again two minutes after the teams turned around.

RANGERS: Foderingham; Tavernier, Wilson, McCrorie, John; Candeias, Jack, Holt, Windass (Kranjcar, 69); Miller, Morelos (Hardie, 85). Subs not used: Alnwick, Herrera, Hodson, Alves, Barjonas.

Rangers 3, Aberdeen 0
Goals: Tavernier (2), Peña

Another convincing home win arrived at the end of November, this time Aberdeen coming off second-best against their on-form hosts.

It was a match Rangers were determined to take three points from and they had their noses in front after just seven minutes. Jason Holt was fouled in the box and James Tavernier stepped up to convert the spot-kick.

The recalled Carlos Peña returned to scoring ways when he netted as the half-hour mark approached and it was a lead the home side were never going to surrender.

In fact, Tavernier added to the Dons' woes with his second of the game 20 minutes from time to complete an impressive victory.

The visitors' night went from bad to worse with Ryan Christie being shown a red card late on.

RANGERS: Foderingham, Tavernier, Wilson, Alves, John; McCrorie, Jack, Holt, Peña (Candeias 68'), Windass (Hardie 87'), Miller (Herrera 83'). Subs not used: Alnwick, Bates, Hodson, Kranjcar.

Saturday 9th December 2017

Rangers 2, Ross County 1
Goals: Morelos, Wilson

The hosts had to dig deep to keep the points at Ibrox but in the end it was another important victory for the Light Blues.

The home fans were stunned when County took a shock lead after just 10 minutes, Craig Curran heading home after good build-up play from Jason Naismith.

Rangers had to wait until the second half to claw themselves back into proceedings, and it was substitute Alfredo Morelos who did the trick with a good finish.

The equaliser put a different feel to the game and with Rangers smelling blood, the winner duly arrived. Josh Windass saw a header well saved by the Staggies' keeper but Danny Wilson was on hand to pounce on the rebound and clinch what was his side's third successive win for the first time in the campaign.

RANGERS: Foderingham; Tavernier, Alves, Wilson, John; McCrorie (Barjonas, 73) Holt, Candeias, Peña (Morelos, 45); Windass, Miller. Subs not used: Kelly, Herrera, Hodson, Kranjcar, Bates.

Sunday 3rd December 2017

Aberdeen 1, Rangers 2
Goals: Wilson, Windass

Just days after beating Aberdeen at Ibrox, Rangers made the trip north to take on the same opponents and emerged victorious once again.

Danny Wilson got things moving in the Granite City after 14 minutes when he met a Declan John cross to send a looping header beyond Joe Lewis.

The Light Blues had to regroup ten minutes after the break after Ryan Jack was shown a straight red but they made light of the numerical disadvantage and stretched their lead after 63 minutes when the on-form Josh Windass netted his fourth goal in six games.

The home side pulled one back through Frank Ross two minutes later but there was to be no denying Rangers the victory which saw them leapfrog Aberdeen into second place.

RANGERS: Foderingham, Tavernier, Bates, Wilson (Cardoso, 45), John, McCrorie, Jack, Holt, Peña (Candeias, 57) Windass (Herrera, 93), Miller. Subs not used: Alnwick, Hodson, Morelos, Barjonas.

Hibs 1, Rangers 2
Goals: Windass, Morelos

Christmas came early for Rangers with a victory at Easter Road which for long spells looked rather unlikely.

Hibs enjoyed a strong grip of the game in the first half and were deserving of the lead given to them by Lewis Stevenson in the ninth minute.

Rangers had Wes Foderingham to thank for keeping them in the match, the keeper foiling both Paul Hanlon and Martin Boyle in quick succession.

Josh Windass handed the Gers a lifeline as the break approached with a terrific finish after good work from Jason Holt. Things got even better for the visitors moments later when Alfredo Morelos turned the game on its head when he shot home to send the Rangers fans wild with delight.

Rangers had to ride their luck after half-time but a combination of poor finishing from Hibs, good goalkeeping by Foderingham and the woodwork saw them hold out for a fourth win on the bounce which kept the momentum going nicely.

RANGERS: Foderingham, Tavernier, Alves, Wilson, John, McCrorie, Holt, Barjonas (Bates, 72), Miller, Windass, Morelos (Herrera, 84). Subs not used: Kelly, Hodson, Kranjcar, Candeias, Peña.

Rangers 2, Motherwell 0
Goals: Wilson, Morelos

Birthday boy Danny Wilson set Rangers on the road to victory when he broke the deadlock early in the second half, his left-foot shot bringing him his third strike of the season.

It was a keenly contested affair at Ibrox with chances being created at both ends of the park.

Alfredo Morelos, however, was the man to convert the one that mattered, his effort 14 minutes from time finally getting the better of Well keeper Carson and clinching an important three points.

RANGERS: Foderingham, Tavernier, Alves, Wilson, John, McCrorie, Jack (Barjonas 41'), Holt, Kranjcar (Peña 83'), Morelos (Hardie 83'), Herrera. Subs not used: Kelly, Hodson, Bates, Candeias.

Celtic 0, Rangers 0

The blank scoreline doesn't tell the full story of this Old Firm clash at Parkhead.

Rangers weren't fancied by many going into the game but they carved out a number of chances throughout the 90 minutes and can count themselves unfortunate to have taken just a point back to Ibrox.

The home side had Craig Gordon to thank for earning them a share of the spoils with the Scotland goalkeeper producing a number of fine stops to keep Rangers at bay.

On another day, the outcome could well have been different but nevertheless it was an encouraging performance to see out the year.

RANGERS: Foderingham, Tavernier, Alves (Bates, 18), Wilson, John, McCrorie, Holt, Windass, Candeias, Kranjcar (Peña, 80), Morelos (Herrera, 88). Subs not used: Alnwick, Hodson, Hardie, Barjonas.

Wednesday 24th January 2018

Rangers 2, Aberdeen 0
Goals: Morelos, Tavernier

It was a special occasion for midfielder Jason Holt, the former Hearts man being handed the captain's armband for the first time and he will long remember the match with the home side sweeping aside the Dons.

A goal in each half from Alfredo Morelos and James Tavernier did the damage as Rangers once again proved too strong for their opponents from the Granite City, the win their third over the Dons in eight weeks.

Morelos converted Tavernier's cross for his 13th goal of the season before his team-mate slotted home a second-half penalty to return Rangers to second place in the Premiership table.

RANGERS: Foderingham, Tavernier, Martin, John, Murphy, Holt, Goss, Candeias (Cardoso, 95'), Windass (Halliday, 89'), Morelos (Cummings, 70'). Subs not used: Alnwick, Hodson, Herrera.

Sunday 28th January 2018

Ross County 1, Rangers 2
Goals: Candeias, Cummings

Loan star Jason Cummings picked the perfect time to notch his first goal for the club, his effort with eight minutes to go proving the difference between the sides.

The striker had only been on the pitch for a matter of minutes when he made his telling contribution, with a left-foot shot into the corner of the net.

Daniel Candeias had put the visitors ahead during a dominant first-half display and although County scored from the spot in the dying seconds, there was to be no denying Rangers a good win on the road.

RANGERS: Foderingham, John, Tavernier, Bates, Murphy, Holt, Goss (Docherty, 74'), Windass, Murphy, Candeias (Halliday, 84'), Morelos (Cummings, 79'). Subs not used: Alnwick, Kranjcar, Cardoso, Herrera.

Tuesday 6th February 2018

Partick Thistle 0, Rangers 2
Goals: Windass, Tavernier

Josh Windass broke the deadlock six minutes from the interval to give Rangers a strong foothold in the game at Firhill.

Having grabbed the initiative they dominated the second period and added a second through James Tavernier's thunderbolt on the hour mark.

Despite some late pressure from the home side, the visitors' defence stood firm to record an important, confidence-boosting clean sheet.

RANGERS: Foderingham, Tavernier, Bates, Martin, John (Halliday 45'), Holt, Goss, Murphy, Windass, Candeias (Docherty 86'), Cummings (Morelos 81').
Subs not used: Alnwick, Cardoso, Miller, Dodoo.

Sunday 18th February 2018

Hamilton Accies 3, Rangers 5
Goals: Murphy, Windass (3), Morelos

Josh Windass was the Rangers hero with a hat-trick as goals rained down at the Superseal Stadium.

In an amazing opening to the game, six goals were scored with just 34 minutes on the clock.

Lyon put the hosts ahead within five minutes, before Jamie Murphy and Windass, with his first strike of the match, had Rangers' noses in front. No sooner had they battled their way into a lead than former Ibrox player David Templeton levelled things in the 22nd minute. As play raged to the other end, Alfredo Morelos restored the Gers' advantage before Windass made it 4-2 in a breathless first half.

Windass then completed his treble 18 minutes from the end but there was still time for Accies to score again, this time Dougie Imrie netting from the spot in the closing stages of a quite enthralling encounter.

RANGERS: Foderingham, Tavernier, Bates, Martin, John, Goss (Halliday 86'), Docherty, Windass (Miller 78'), Candeias, Murphy, Morelos (Cummings 78') Subs not used: Kelly, Hodson, Cardoso, Herrera.

Saturday 24th February 2018

Rangers 2, Hearts 0
Goals: Murphy, Martin

Jamie Murphy notched his first goal for the club when he put Rangers ahead as the half-time interval approached, his finish from Greg Docherty's pass producing a deafening roar from the home supporters.

Rangers went on to dominate the second period but only had one other goal to account for all their pressure, and that arrived with just two minutes remaining via the unlikely figure of Russell Martin, who slid in at the back post to make the game safe.

RANGERS: Foderingham; Tavernier, Martin, Bates, John; Docherty, (Holt, 83') Goss; Candeias, Windass, Murphy; Morelos (Cummings, 73'). Subs not used: Alnwick, Miller, Herrera, Halliday, Alves.

Tuesday 27th February 2018

St Johnstone 1, Rangers 4
Goals: Tavernier, Windass, Goss, Morelos

The month of February continued to prove a good one for the Light Blues, with Rangers easing to their fifth straight win of the campaign against St Johnstone.

In difficult wintry conditions, James Tavernier broke the deadlock from the penalty spot before Josh Windass and Sean Goss had Rangers on easy street by half-time.

After the turnaround, Alfredo Morelos got on the scoresheet yet again and even a late goal from Saints' Jason Kerr failed to dampen the mood of the Rangers squad as they headed home from Perth.

RANGERS: Foderingham, Tavernier, Bates, Martin, Halliday, Goss, Docherty, Murphy (Alves 77'), Windass, Candeias (Cummings 62'), Morelos. Subs not used: Alnwick, Herrera, Holt, Miller, Hodson.

Saturday 31st March 2017

Motherwell 2, Rangers 2
Goals: Tavernier, Murphy

A performance of some determination was required as Rangers fought back from two goals down to earn a share of the spoils at Fir Park.

Two down in less than 20 minutes through goals from Chris Main and Allan Campbell, it was not the start the visitors had wanted but thanks to an impressive second half, they travelled back to Ibrox with something to show for their efforts.

James Tavernier converted from the spot six minutes after the interval and two minutes later the game was tied, Jamie Murphy shooting home the equaliser.

RANGERS: Foderingham, Tavernier, Alves, Martin, John, Docherty, Dorrans, Candeias, Windass (Cummings 81'), Murphy, Morelos. Subs not used: Alnwick, Hodson, Halliday, Miller, McCrorie, Goss.

Sunday 22nd April 2018

Rangers 2, Hearts 1
Goals: Cummimgs, Candeias

Despite the narrow margin of victory, there could be little doubt the home side deserved their victory over the Jambos.

Jason Cummings handed the hosts the advantage when he broke the deadlock two minutes into the second half, the striker slotting home from inside the six-yard box.

Daniel Candeias netted a second as Hearts struggled to keep Rangers, now full of confidence, at bay and although Christophe Berra pulled one back for the Edinburgh outfit, the final whistle brought rapturous applause from the Govan faithful as they celebrated a good win.

RANGERS: Alnwick; Tavernier, Martin, McCrorie, John; Dorrans, Holt; Candeias (O'Halloran, 90'), Windass, (Halliday 76'), Murphy; Cummings (Morelos, 86'). Subs not used: Kelly, Hodson, Goss, Docherty.

Saturday 7th April 2018

Rangers 4, Dundee 0
Goals: Miller, Morelos, Murphy, Candeias

It's never easy playing against a team fighting for survival but Rangers comfortably saw off the challenge of Neil McCann's Dundee strugglers.

A goal from Kenny Miller had the hosts ahead at the interval and they gave themselves some breathing space in the match when Alfredo Morelos doubled the advantage midway through the second period.

Although Dundee battled valiantly, Jamie Murphy made the points safe with a goal 11 minutes from time before Daniel Candeias put the icing on the cake in the closing moments.

RANGERS: Foderingham; Tavernier, McCrorie (Alves 65'), Martin, John; Docherty (Halliday 61'), Dorrans; Candeias, Miller (Goss 78'), Murphy; Morelos. Subs not used: Alnwick, Hodson, Cummings, O'Halloran.

Saturday 5th May 2018

Rangers 1, Kilmarnock 0
Goals: Bates

With the visit of Kilmarnock coming a day after Steven Gerrard was unveiled as the new manager of Rangers, it was a buoyant crowd which greeted the players from the tunnel.

The fans had to be patient, however, as their team set about unlocking a well organised Killie defence, the Ayrshire side themselves having been transformed since the arrival of Steve Clarke.

One goal was enough to settle the match, and it was David Bates who popped up with the all-important strike five minutes from time when he bundled the ball home at the back post.

RANGERS: Alnwick, Tavernier, Dorrans, Halliday, Morelos, Candeias, Holt (Goss, 74'), Bates, Cummings (McCrorie, 45'), Murphy, Martin. Subs not used: Kelly, Hodson, Rossiter, Alves, Docherty.

Tuesday 8th May 2018

Aberdeen 1, Rangers 1
Goals: McCrorie

Youngster Ross McCrorie rode to Rangers' rescue at Pittodrie, scoring the all-important equaliser as the Light Blues salvaged a battling point from their trip to the Granite City.

The visitors had fallen behind to a Kenny McLean spot-kick in the first half but they were in no mood to taste defeat in their penultimate match of the season.

With 63 minutes on the clock McCrorie got the better of Joe Lewis in the Aberdeen goal. It was his second strike for the club and set Rangers up well for their trip to Easter Road on the final day of the campaign.

RANGERS: Alnwick; Tavernier, Martin, Bates, Halliday; McCrorie, Holt (Cummings, 60'); Candeias, Dorrans (Goss, 33'), Murphy; Morelos. Subs not used: Kelly, Hodson, Rossiter, Alves, Docherty.

Sunday 13th May 2018

Sunday 13th May 2018

Hibs 5, Rangers 5
Goals: Tavernier, Rossiter, Alves, Holt, Windass

The final game of season will long be remembered by those who witnessed the amazing scenes at Easter Road, with ten goals being shared on an afternoon of quite incredible drama.

The home side came out of the traps like possessed greyhounds and remarkably had raced into a 3-0 lead within 22 minutes.

Rangers could well have buckled under the pressure of such a start but to their immense credit, the Light Blues staged an impressive fightback to take the lead in Leith.

James Tavernier scored in the 25th minute and two minutes later teammate Jordan Rossiter found the back of the net to breathe new life into the Gers. With 39 minutes gone, the visitors had cancelled out the Hibees' advantage when Bruno Alves smashed home a stunning free-kick.

A capacity Easter Road could scarcely believe what they were watching and the action was far from finished!

Ten minutes after the restart and Rangers were in front, Jason Holt applying the finishing touches to Jamie Murphy's cross. With 68 minutes on the clock, Rangers went further ahead, this time Holt's shot being deflected past Marciano by Josh Windass. Barely 45 minutes after falling 3-0 behind, Rangers were now 5-3 in front.

There was yet more drama to come, Hibs hitting back seconds later through Maclaren. Five minutes from the end, Holt picked up a second yellow card and the sending off was to prove crucial as Hibs managed to snatch an injury-time equaliser through Maclaren to bring the curtain down on a sensational afternoon of football.

RANGERS: Alnwick; Tavernier, Martin, Bates, Halliday; Rossiter (Hodson, 68'), Goss (Alves, 28'), Holt; Candeias, Cummings (Windass, 62'), Murphy. Subs not used: Kelly, Herrera, O'Halloran, Docherty.

RANGERS

20 QUESTIONS

1 How many caps did Steven Gerrard win for England?

2 What club did Gerrard work for before joining Rangers?

3 How many words appear on the club crest?

4 What are they?

5 Who scored Rangers' first league goal last season?

6 And who was the opposition?

7 In what year was Rangers formed?

8 Ibrox is located in which area of Glasgow?

9 How many goals did Rangers score last season in the league?

10 Who was Gerrard's first signing as manager?

11 At what stadium did Rangers play their final league game of 2017/18?

12 How many points did the Light Blues finish on last season?

13 Can you name Rangers' goalkeeping coach?

14 What is the postcode of Ibrox Stadium?

15 How many Scotland caps did Gary McAllister win?

16 Which Scottish clubs has Allan McGregor played for?

17 True or False: Steven Gerrard began working as Rangers manager in May 2018.

18 Mark Hateley left which country to move to Rangers?

19 What roles does Jordan Milsom play at the club?

20 Ovie Ejaria joined Rangers on loan from which club?

Answers on page 61.

RANGERS
SOCCER SCHOOLS

Train & Play
The Rangers Way!

Rangers Soccer Schools offer participants the chance
to experience fun-filled sessions with a range of
options suitable for all ages and abilities.

For more information or to book
call **0871 702 1972*** (option 4) or email **soccerschools@rangers.co.uk**

*calls cost 13p per minute plus network extras

SPOT THE BALL P17

CROSSWORD P28

						F											
A						E					S					
L	I	G	H	T	B	L	U	E	S	C			M	A	Y	
N						E				S	C	O	T	T		
W						T					O			B		A
I						W					T			R		B
C				M		O					T			O		E
K				A		O						B		X		R
				L								R				D
		S	A	N	D	Y	J	A	R	D	I	N	E			E
				A								G				N
		H	A	M	M	E	R		B			H		S		
									R			T		P		
G	O	V	A	N		S	C	O	T	L	A	N	D	A		
									O					I		
		W	H	I	S	T	O	N	N					N		

20 QUESTIONS P59

1. 114 2. Liverpool 3. 4 4. Rangers, Football, Club, Ready 5. Graham Dorrans 6. Motherwell 7. 1873 8. Govan 9. 76 10. Scott Arfield 11. Easter Road 12. 70 13. Colin Stewart 14. G51 2XD 15. 57 16. Rangers, St Johnstone, Dunfermline 17. False. His first day at the office was June 1st 2018. 18. France 19. Head of Performance 20. Liverpool

GUESS WHO? P28

Ross McCrorie   James Tavernier   Daniel Candeias   Serge Atakayi

PLAYERS P16
WORDSEARCH

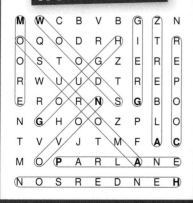

RANGERS P38
WORDSEARCH

MAZE P46

61

WHERE'S BROXI?